Have You Met My Daddy by Butch Bruton will warm your heart like mail from home. Butch has written a letter about his loving Father that every believer should read. It turns out he's writing about my Father, too. Thanks, Butch, for writing the truth about my Daddy.

—Kenneth Copeland

HAVE YOU MET MY DADDY?

*Discover the Loving and
Compassionate Heavenly Father*

BY
BUTCH BRUTON

HARRISON HOUSE
Tulsa, Oklahoma

14 13 12 11   10 9 8 7 6 5 4

Have You Met My Daddy?
Discover the Loving and Compassionate Heavenly Father
ISBN 10: 1-57794-912-9
ISBN 13: 978-1-57794-912-1
Copyright © 2008 by Butch Bruton
PO Box 787
Caddo Mills, TX 75135
www.nlff.org

Published by Harrison House, Inc.
PO Box 35035
Tulsa, Oklahoma 74153
www.harrisonhouse.com

TABLE OF CONTENTS

FOREWORD

I would like to introduce you to a wonderful book called *Have You Met My Daddy?* by Butch Bruton. If there is one thing I've learned about living for the Lord Jesus Christ, it is that if you're going to have a happy Christian life, you've got to see God as a Father and see yourself as part of His family, and not as part of some institution—cold, callused, and uncompassionate to our needs. As you'll read in this book, our Heavenly Father (our Daddy) wants to "protect, provide for, increase, and enjoy His children, just as any good daddy does." In fact, you'll learn that God considers it not only His job but His greatest responsibility!

I love this book because it really cuts to the chase and shows you just how personal you can become with the Lord Jesus Christ and with our Heavenly Father. I especially liked the story about the two young sisters who don't look alike but say they're twins—one was adopted, but they didn't know the difference. And you know, God sees us the same way because of Jesus! Glory!

So sit down and enjoy yourself, because when you finish this book, I believe you will have a closer relationship with God than you ever thought possible. Butch will show you how you can do that through the simple technique of loving your Father. This book will open your eyes to see how good our Daddy really is and I believe it will change your life.

Enjoy the read—I certainly did!

—Jesse Duplantis

Introduction

A few months ago, I was watching a video of two friends skeet shooting. The young men, both very good shooters, had decided to test their skills against each other. The first young man said, "If I hit the most clays and win, I get to shoot that brand new cowboy hat you're wearing."

The other young man laughed and replied, "OK, but what do I get if I win?"

Without thinking the first guy said, "Well, if you win, my daddy will give you $200."

I listened to the bet, curious to see what his father would do. As the camera turned toward his father, he sat there nodding and grinning in approval, ready to watch his son compete. He gladly supported his son's bet because he was a daddy who was going to back his kid, no matter what; and you could tell he had done it before.

As I thought about what I had seen, I began to think about our Heavenly Father. We use the term "Heavenly Father" a lot, but do we really know what that means? We have been taught all our lives that Jesus is loving, compassionate, and caring; but when it comes to His Father, our Heavenly Father, we often see him as stern, strict, and a force that will get you if you are not living right. That's wrong thinking and it isn't the true nature of our God. The Bible says that Jesus is the express image of the Father. (Heb. 1:3; 2 Cor. 4:4.) The same love and compassion that Jesus walked in is how our Heavenly Father operates toward us, His children.

We have all seen and heard young kids bragging about their daddies. One might say, "Well my daddy is so strong, he can pick up 500 pounds." Another might argue, "Well my daddy is so rich, he is going to buy me that new bike."

Whether or not we grew up with a first-rate dad, deep inside all of us is a knowing of what a good daddy should be. He is one who has the ability and means to do it all and who has the love and compassion to do it for his children. Our Heavenly Father wants to be "My Daddy" to each of us. He wants to be our provider and protector, but for too long we have denied him that right. As we learn more about the nature of God and how to accept Him as Daddy, we can begin to walk in the love, provision, and protection He so desires for us. Through Jesus, we are His children, and He wants to be our Daddy!

Chapter 1

ABBA FATHER

I once heard a story of two young sisters, who were in the same class and grade at school. This puzzled their teacher because the girls looked nothing alike, and it was unlikely they were twins. Curious, the teacher finally questioned both of the young girls.

She asked, "How is it that you two are sisters, are the same age and in the same grade but look nothing alike? I just can't believe that you are twins." The young girls looked at each other and smiled. One girl replied, "Teacher, that's easy. One of us is adopted, but I forget which one."

In Romans 8:14,15, the Bible says, "For as many as are led by the Spirit of God, they are the sons of God. For ye have not received the spirit of bondage again to fear; but ye have received the Spirit of adoption whereby we cry, Abba, Father." In our society, stories like that of the two young sisters are rare. Adoption can be hard for some, but not so with God.

When we were adopted into the family of God through Jesus, we were made complete sons and daughters. Just like in the story of the two girls, God our father loves us the same as He loves Jesus. We are joint heirs with our big brother Jesus.

Galatians 4:6 says, "And because ye are sons, God hath sent forth the Spirit of his Son into your hearts, crying, Abba, Father." The phrase "Abba Father" used in both scripture references can be translated back to the Greek phrase meaning vocation. God's talking about his primary vocation, which is being our Father.

He just wants to be Daddy, and He considers that his greatest responsibility. His job or profession, according to His Word, is to be Daddy to his children. He wants to protect, provide for, increase, and enjoy his children, just as any good daddy does. He has even provided us with the Spirit of His Son, which cries, "Abba Father" or "Daddy".

Chapter 2

What Would You Do?

Imagine for a minute that you have it all. You own beautiful mansions around the world. You have billions of dollars at your disposal. You drive the nicest cars and take the most luxurious vacations. You are the richest of the rich and are known for your generous nature.

Now in that imagination, how do you picture your children? Do they share in your wealth, or must they beg and plead to get their basic needs met? Are they joint owners and CEOs in the family business, or do they spend their days begging in the streets? If you had it all, what would your kids have?

Matthew 7:9-11 says, "Or what man is there of you, whom if his son ask bread, will he give him a stone? Or if he ask a fish, will give him a serpent? If ye then, being evil, know how to give good gifts unto your children, how much more shall your Father which is in heaven give good things to them that ask him?"

If you had it all, you would not think twice about loading your children with all the luxuries that money could buy. In fact, you would take great pleasure to see that not only their needs were met but their wants as well. That's how we should think about our Heavenly Father, the Daddy of all daddies.

He is the richest of the rich, and not only in wealth; He is the richest in peace, the richest in health, the richest in wisdom, and the richest in love. He truly has it all, yet Christians (his children) daily refuse to accept what He has provided for His kids.

Many have never believed or received Him as the loving and good Daddy that He is. They either assume that it is His will that they live in lack, or they spend their time begging in fear and unbelief.

In the natural, men would be arrested for treating their children the way God is often accused of treating His. If a child were starved, broken, beaten, and crushed in an attempt to teach the child a lesson, the father would be arrested and charged with multiple accounts of child abuse.

We know this is not the way to treat our children. Why then, do we accuse our

Heavenly Father of doing these things in the natural realm? A good father blesses, encourages, and loves his child. God is the ultimate Father and his goodness toward His children can't be measured.

We must begin to use our faith in believing that our Heavenly Father is our gracious, loving, all-powerful Daddy. If natural, evil (or sinful) men can graciously provide for their children, how much more does our Heavenly Father, our Daddy, provide for us!

Chapter 3

I Am That…I Am!

In Exodus 3 Moses is talking with God on the mountain. He asks God who he should say is sending him to deliver the Israelites out of the hand of the Egyptians. Moses asks, "…Behold, when I come unto the children of Israel, and shall say unto them, The God of your fathers hath sent me unto you; and they shall say to me, What is his name? what shall I say unto them?" (Ex. 3:13). God answers, "I AM THAT I AM…Thus shalt thou say unto the children of Israel, I AM hath sent me unto you."

He was telling Moses and the Children of Israel that whatever they needed, He was. He was saying whatever you need, I am THAT. Healing, I AM *THAT*, I AM. Deliverance, I AM *THAT*, I AM. Peace, wholeness, safety, I AM *THAT*, I AM.

The fact was, He was the I AM for the Children of Israel since the covenant was made with their forefather, Abraham, but they did not receive Him as their deliverer until the time of Moses. They walked in horrible, continual bondage until they received their God as their "I AM THAT."

Because God is the same yesterday, today, and forever, His "I AM THAT" title remains true forever. In fact, it is even truer for us now because we are sons and daughters of God through Jesus and not just children of His covenant friend Abraham.

He is the I AM, and He wants to fulfill His role of all sufficient provider and protector in our lives. He wants to be the "I AM THAT" Daddy. When His children need peace, He says, "I AM THAT." When His children need love, He says, "I AM THAT." When His children need wealth, He says, "I AM THAT." He is the daddy who has it all and wants His children to be full partakers.

Chapter 4

WHO DO YOU SAY THAT "I AM"?

There is one condition to receiving from the "I AM" nature of God. You must first believe that He is the "I AM" Daddy, and then you must believe that His greatest desire is to be your "I AM" Daddy. You cannot receive Him as Daddy if you fear Him as a God who will make you suffer with lack and sickness or who will teach you a lesson through pain and loss. That is not the nature of God, our Daddy.

He is good all the time and uses His Word to instruct His children. You must walk in faith, knowing that God is love. He is the ultimate Daddy who uses nothing but good things when dealing with His children. For many this means having to uproot years of wrong information, wrong thinking, and wrong beliefs regarding the nature of God. He is the I AM and wants His children to walk fully in His love, wealth, health, peace, and life without sorrow, loss, or pain.

Your unbelief or wrong belief does not change who God is; it changes who He can be for you. In Matthew 16:15 Jesus asked His disciples, "...But whom say ye that I am?" or who do you say that I am? It does not matter what others around you are saying about God. He is asking you, "Who do *you* say that I am?" He wants to know who you say He is.

Will you receive Him as the healer that He is? Will you receive Him as the provider that He is? Will you receive Him as the Daddy that He is? You must decide to believe, say, and receive God as Daddy—the ultimate Daddy, the "I AM" Daddy. You must receive Him as the Daddy who always loves, blesses, gives to, provides for, uplifts, and enjoys His children. He's the greatest Daddy that ever was or will be.

Chapter 5

My Daddy…Is He Yours?

Throughout this book, we have referred to God as the ultimate Daddy, but the truth is He can only be Daddy to those who are born again through Jesus. Without accepting the covenant sacrifice Jesus provided, you cannot live in the protection and provision that God has promised and given to His children. Without being born again, you are living outside of the family. However, the good news is that through a simple prayer spoken in faith, you can become a son or daughter of God and receive the wonderful blessings discussed throughout this book.

In Romans 10:9, 13 the Bible says, "…if thou shalt confess with thy mouth the Lord Jesus, and shalt believe in thine heart that God hath raised him from the dead, thou shalt be saved. For whosoever shall call upon the name of the Lord shall be saved." You now can become a child of the ultimate Daddy! He says that he who comes to Him, He will in no way cast out. He wants to be Daddy to you.

SALVATION PRAYER

Heavenly Father, I ask you today to be my Daddy. Jesus, I believe that you died and rose again for me, and I ask you to come into my heart and be my Savior. Please forgive me of all my sins and fill me with your Holy Spirit. Thank you, Heavenly Father, for being My Daddy and receiving me as your child. In Jesus name, I pray, amen.

If you prayed this prayer to receive Jesus Christ as your Savior for the first time, please contact us on the web at **www.harrisonhouse.com** to receive a free book.

Or you may write to us at

Harrison House
PO Box 35035
Tulsa, Oklahoma 74153

DECLARATIONS OF FAITH TO YOUR FATHER

Becoming the Person God Says I Am

I choose to live a godly life before my family and friends. I am disciplined concerning the priorities of my life. I manage my time in an effective and efficient manner. I am sensitive to the needs of my family and friends. I have God's wisdom and discernment concerning all my decisions.

I am loving, caring, and compassionate toward others. I keep my cool during times of stress and do not become frustrated and lose my temper. If I do something that is wrong or offensive, I am quick to repent. Because I live a Spirit-controlled life, I am peaceful, consistent, and faithful. I walk in love at all times, and I am quick to provide encouragement and inspiration to those who need it.

I know the voice of the Holy Spirit, and I am quick to obey His voice. God's presence and peace adorn my life like a beautiful gown. God's grace and favor are a crown upon my head. His goodness and mercy follow me all the days of my life.

Scriptures

…we should live soberly, righteously, and godly, in this present world.

Titus 2:12

If any of you lack wisdom, let him ask of God, that giveth to all men liberally, and upbraideth not; and it shall be given him.

James 1:5

…be thou an example of the believers, in word, in conversation, in charity, in spirit, in faith, in purity.

1 Timothy 4:12

Healing for My Body

I proclaim healing for my body. By Jesus' stripes I am healed. The healing, life-giving, disease-destroying power of God is working in my body. It drives out all manner of sickness and disease. I am full of life, health, strength, and vitality. I am healthy and whole from the top of my head to the soles of my feet.

Every organ in my body operates and functions the way God created it to with no disease or malfunctions. Every system in my body operates and functions with supernatural efficiency. My nervous system, lymphatic system, digestive system, electrical system, circulatory system, and every other system functions with 100 percent efficiency.

Jesus Himself bore my sickness and carried my diseases; therefore, sickness and disease are not allowed to exist in my body. My body is free from growths, tumors, or obstructions of any kind.

The divine *zoe* life of God flows through me, quickening and making alive my mortal body. My body is free from pain, discomfort, distress, and all symptoms of sickness. God's Word is medicine to my flesh. I am not moved by how I feel, how I look, or any negative reports, because I believe God's Word and His Word says I am healed. I am healed, healthy, and whole in Jesus' name.

Scriptures

But he was wounded for our transgressions, he was bruised for our iniquities: the chastisement of our peace was upon him; and with his stripes we are healed.

Isaiah 53:5

My son, attend to my words; incline thine ear unto my sayings. Let them not depart from thine eyes; keep them in the midst of thine heart. For they are life unto those that find them, and health to all their flesh.

Proverbs 4:20-22

He sent his word, and healed them, and delivered them from their destructions.

Psalm 107:20

That it might be fulfilled which was spoken by Esaias the prophet, saying, Himself took our infirmities, and bare our sicknesses.

Matthew 8:17

Who his own self bare our sins in his own body on the tree, that we, being dead to sins, should live unto righteousness: by whose stripes ye were healed.

1 Peter 2:24

God Is My Source

My God supplies all my needs according to His riches in glory. It is God's will that I prosper. He is Jehovah-Jireh, my provider. Jesus was made poor that I might become rich. I am blessed by the Lord; and if I honor Him, He will honor me. Wealth and riches are in my house. The Lord is my shepherd; He takes care of me. Therefore, I shall not suffer from want or lack anything. I do not fear, I am not troubled or anxious, and I do not worry about my finances.

I know that God takes care of the birds and the flowers, and I am much more important to Him than they are. Since I know that He takes care of them, I know He will take good care of me. Therefore, I will not worry about where I will get the money I need for the necessities of life such as food, rent, car payments, clothes, or mortgage payments. My job is not my source, my relatives are not my source, and my credit cards are not my source. God is my source of supply, and He will never let me down.

Scriptures

My God shall supply all your need according to his riches in glory by Christ Jesus.

Philippians 4:19

Ye know the grace of our Lord Jesus Christ, that, though he was rich, yet for your sakes he became poor, that ye through his poverty might be rich.

2 Corinthians 8:9

Even the very hairs of your head are all numbered. Fear not therefore: ye are of more value than many sparrows.

Luke 12:7

Humility and the fear of the LORD bring wealth and honor and life.

Proverbs 22:4 NIV

Peace

God has given me His peace, not peace that comes from worldly sources but a supernatural, divine peace. God's peace is a spiritual force that passes all natural reasoning and understanding. I will not allow my heart to be troubled, worried, or fearful, for I have God's peace in me. His peace keeps me cool, calm, and collected no matter what I am faced with. God's peace gives me the ability to remain level-headed and resolute in the face of misfortune and calamity.

His peace is the umpire of my soul; it garrisons and mounts guard over my heart and mind. God's peace keeps me from becoming fretful and anxious over situations in my life. He helps me to remain steady and unruffled when I face challenges and adversity. God's peace gives me confidence and surety that God is working for me, with me, and in me to fulfill His plan and purpose for my life. I can face the uncertainty of the future without apprehension and with complete confidence, knowing that God will work all things out for my good.

Scriptures

Thou wilt keep him in perfect peace, whose mind is stayed on thee: because he trusteth in thee.

Isaiah 26:3

For the mountains shall depart, and the hills be removed; but my kindness shall not depart from thee, neither shall the covenant of my peace be removed, saith the LORD that hath mercy on thee.

Isaiah 54:10

Peace I leave with you, my peace I give unto you: not as the world giveth, give I unto you. Let not your heart be troubled, neither let it be afraid.

John 14:27

And the peace of God, which passeth all understanding, shall keep your hearts and minds through Christ Jesus.

Philippians 4:7

Divine Protection

God's Word promises divine protection for the children of God. Therefore I proclaim that no evil shall come near me or my family. No plague shall come near our home; though a thousand may fall at my side and ten thousand at my right hand, it shall not, will not, cannot come near me or my family.

God's angels encamp around about us. God has given His angels charge over us to protect us and keep us from danger, harm, and injury of any kind.

Though I walk through the fire I will not be burned. If I find myself in flood waters, they will not overtake me. Though I walk through the valley of the shadow of death, I will fear no evil, for God is with me. No weapon formed against me shall prosper.

God is my refuge and my fortress. God will deliver me from the traps of the enemy, and He will deliver me from deadly diseases. Under God's wings I take refuge and His truth is my shield and my protection from all the dangers of this world.

Scriptures

Let your conversation be without covetousness; and be content with such things as ye have: for he hath said, I will never leave thee, nor forsake thee.

Hebrews 13:5

Keep me as the apple of the eye, hide me under the shadow of thy wings.

Psalm 17:8

There shall no evil befall thee, neither shall any plague come nigh thy dwelling.

Psalm 91:10

And the peace of God, which passeth all understanding, shall keep your hearts and minds through Christ Jesus.

Philippians 4:7

Favor

I am blessed and highly favored with God and with man. The favor of God is operating and functioning in my life. It surrounds my life as a shield. His favor goes before me and prepares my way. Favor opens doors of blessing and opportunity in my life. Wherever I go and whatever I do, God's favor is with me and on me.

God's favor is operating and functioning in every area of my life. I have favor with my family, on my job, and in all of my relationships. All my endeavors are blessed. God's blessings of favor come to me every day. Whatever I set my hand to prospers and succeeds because of His favor.

God's favor brings promotion and increase to my life. God's favor fills my life with overflowing blessing, peace, joy, fulfillment, and abundance. God's favor takes me where my own ability and wisdom cannot. Wonderful things are always happening to me, so it's a surety that something good is going to happen to me today.

Scriptures

A good man obtaineth favour of the Lord: but a man of wicked devices will he condemn.

Proverbs 12:2

When a man's ways please the LORD, he maketh even his enemies to be at peace with him.

Proverbs 16:7

For thou, Lord, wilt bless the righteous; with favour wilt thou compass him as with a shield.

Psalm 5:12

I know thy works: behold, I have set before thee an open door, and no man can shut it....

Revelation 3:8

About the Author

Pastor's Butch and Darlene Bruton have been pastoring the congregation at New Life Family Fellowship since the Church began in 1987. They have chosen to preach the uncompromised Word of God and proclaim to the world that God is Good and He is Good All The Time!

Accepting the call of God on his life in 1972, he has been in the ministry for over 25 years. In 1987, he retired from 15 years as a firefighter and went into the ministry full time. Since then he has preached the Word of God in countries around the world.

In 1994, God placed in Pastor Butch's heart the vision of Covenant Ranch. As president and founder, he has watched the dream of God unfold. Covenant Ranch is a place where people can come to rest their flesh and increase their faith. God is doing a mighty work in Caddo Mills, Texas. With a covered arena, concession stand, and ranch store, the vision and ministry of Covenant Ranch is growing rapidly.

Pastor's Butch and Darlene believe that there is only good news to tell. People need to know that God is their answer, not their problem. At New Life, Covenant Ranch, and in countries around the world, they are proclaiming that God is good all the time, and one word from Him can change your life forever.

To contact Pastor Bruton please write to:
New Life Church
P.O. Box 787 • Caddo Mills, TX 75135
Telephone: 903-527-3099
Email: nlfforg@nlff.org

Or visit him on the web at: **www.nlff.org**

*Please include your prayer requests
and comments when you write.*

Made in the USA
Monee, IL
26 May 2026